AFFIRMATIONS FOR RECOVERY THE GUIDE

By
Erick D. Allen Sr.

Using the Affirmations For Recovery "The Guide"

Affirmations For Recovery "The Guide" is a publication designed to assist individuals new to recovery and the process of change. Forming new habits requires discipline, commitment, consistency, and most importantly TIME. Studies show it takes 21-30 days to form new habits; 'Recovery is a journey NOT a destination."

This Guide was created to assist with Affirmations for Recovery "The Journal" and offer additional explanation on the word of the day. It will also provide encouragement and motivation along the journey to recovery.

For the next thirty (30) days, be encouraged to change how you speak to and about yourself. Journaling is a great way to identify areas that you want to change and allows the writer the opportunity to reflect on the process. Take as much time as you need daily to explore thoughts, feelings and emotions. Learning how to express yourself is a key component to recovery.

Recovery is a mindset, starting with Day #1; read the passage of the day and write down your thoughts and how you're feeling.

Dedication

I have witness first-hand the power and pain associated with addiction. I dedicate this Guide to the individuals new to the recovery process.

My family life was a huge inspiration to do this work and I am dedicating the rest of my life to adding 'value' to the recovery community.

I thank GOD, my wife Talibah, L.I.E. Foundation for their continuous support

Day 1
R.E.C.O.V.E.R.

"Recovery
Is Essential"

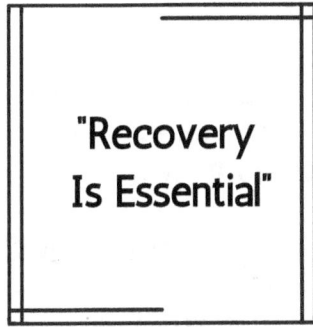

Relentless Encourage Content Optimistic Values
Educate Respect

Recovery is a journey that requires unwavering
support, positivity, and guidance.

The acronym RECOVER embodies these crucial
elements:

Relentless Encouragement
Recovery often involves overcoming obstacles
and setbacks. Providing relentless
encouragement ensures individuals feel
supported and motivated to persevere through
challenges.

Contentment
Finding contentment in the present moment can
be powerful during recovery. It involves
accepting one's circumstances and focusing on

progress rather than dwelling on past mistakes or regrets.

Optimistic Outlook
Maintaining a positive mindset is essential for overcoming adversity. An optimistic outlook enables individuals to see possibilities for growth and change, even in the face of difficult circumstances.

Values-based Approach
Recovery is an opportunity to reevaluate personal values and priorities. By aligning actions with core values, individuals can create a meaningful and fulfilling life beyond addiction or loss.

Education
Knowledge empowers individuals to make informed decisions and develop healthy coping strategies. Education about addiction, grief, or other challenges equips individuals with the tools they need to navigate recovery successfully.

Respect
Respect for oneself and others is fundamental to the recovery process. It involves treating oneself with kindness and compassion, as well as showing empathy and understanding towards others who may be on a similar journey.

In every stage of recovery, whether from substance abuse, loss, or other hardships, embracing the principles of RECOVER can provide a solid foundation for growth and healing. By fostering a supportive environment, promoting self-awareness, and encouraging positive change, RECOVER helps individuals reclaim their lives and move forward with renewed hope and purpose.

*REMEMBER everything starts with a thought, keeping your thoughts 'positive' will lead to better outcomes.

LOOK at this as the FIRST Day of the Rest of your life, change happens when you work for it.

RECOVERY
IS A
JOURNEY
NOT A
DESIGNATION

Day 2
A.C.C.E.P.T.A.N.C.E

"Acceptance is Key to Recovery"

Active Communication Created Experiences People Truly Appreciate Now Choose Empowerment

During the recovery journey, embracing the principles of ACCEPTANCE can lead to profound personal growth and healing:

Active Communication
Open and honest communication is essential for building supportive relationships and addressing underlying issues. By actively engaging in communication, individuals can express their needs, fears, and aspirations, fostering understanding and connection with others.

Created Experiences
Recovery offers an opportunity to create new, positive experiences that contribute to personal fulfillment and well-being. By actively seeking

out enriching activities and relationships, individuals can replace old habits with healthy alternatives, nurturing a sense of purpose and joy.

People Truly Appreciate
Recovery often involves reevaluating relationships and recognizing the value of genuine connections. By cultivating gratitude and appreciation for the people who support them, individuals can strengthen their support network and experience deeper emotional fulfillment.

Now Choose Empowerment
Recovery is ultimately a journey of self-discovery and empowerment. By embracing the power of choice in the present moment, individuals can take control of their lives and make decisions that align with their values and aspirations.

No matter the challenges individuals face during recovery, whether it's overcoming addiction, navigating grief, or rebuilding after a loss, practicing ACCEPTANCE can provide a roadmap for personal transformation and resilience. By actively engaging in communication, creating meaningful experiences, appreciating supportive relationships, and choosing empowerment, individuals can reclaim their lives and build a brighter future filled with hope and possibility.

Serenity Prayer: GOD allow me the strength to except the things I can not change, the courage to change what I can, and the wisdom to know the difference.

There is power in prayer IF YOU Believe!

GOD grant us the SERENITY to accept the things we cannot change, the COURAGE to change the things we can, and the WISDOM to know the difference.

Day 3

A.W.A.K.E.N.I.N.G

"I am awakening to new thoughts!

Apply Wisdom And Knowledge Equals New Insight Now Grow

In the journey of recovery, embracing the principles of AWAKENING can lead to profound personal transformation and growth:

Apply Wisdom and Knowledge
Recovery often involves learning from past experiences and gaining insight into oneself and one's circumstances. By applying wisdom and knowledge gained through education, therapy, or support groups, individuals can make informed decisions and navigate their recovery journey with greater clarity and understanding.

Equals New Insight
The process of recovery opens the door to new perspectives and insights. By embracing curiosity and openness to new ideas, individuals

can gain fresh insights into themselves and their relationships, leading to deeper self-awareness and personal growth.

Now Grow
Recovery is an ongoing process of growth and self-improvement. By embracing the present moment and focusing on personal development, individuals can cultivate resilience and strength, enabling them to overcome challenges and build a fulfilling life beyond addiction, loss, or hardship

No matter the obstacles individuals face during recovery, whether it's overcoming addiction, coping with loss, or rebuilding after a setback, practicing AWAKENING can empower them to tap into their inner wisdom, gain new insights, and embark on a journey of self-discovery and growth. By applying knowledge, seeking new insights, and embracing opportunities for growth, individuals can awaken to their full potential and create a life filled with meaning, purpose, and resilience.

Forming NEW habits require 21-30 days e patient with yourself

Day 4

B.E.L.I.E.V.E

> "I am awakening to new thoughts!"

Bringing Eternal Light Into Existence Validates Eternity

BELIEVE encapsulates the essence of hope and resilience, offering invaluable support during the recovery journey:

Bringing Eternal Light Into Existence
Recovery is often a journey from darkness to light, from despair to hope. By believing in the possibility of a brighter future and actively working towards it, individuals can illuminate their path to recovery and create a life filled with purpose and fulfillment

Validates Eternity
Recovery is a testament to the enduring strength of the human spirit. By believing in one's inherent worth and potential for growth,

individuals can validate their own journey and recognize the eternal value of their efforts to overcome adversity and create positive change.

No matter the challenges individuals face during recovery, whether it's battling addiction, coping with loss, or rebuilding after setbacks, BELIEVE serves as a beacon of hope and inspiration. By embracing the belief in oneself and the possibility of a better tomorrow, individuals can navigate the ups and downs of recovery with courage, resilience, and determination.

Day 5

C.O.M.M.U.N.I.C.A.T.E

"I am awakening to new thoughts!

Creating Opportunities Motivates Meaningful Understanding Not Influence Change And Trust Each Other Effective communication is the cornerstone of successful recovery, and the principles of

COMMUNICATE provide a roadmap for building strong, supportive relationships:

Creating Opportunities
Recovery is a journey of growth and transformation, and effective communication creates opportunities for individuals to express themselves, share their experiences, and connect with others who understand their struggles. By creating these opportunities, individuals can build a sense of community and belonging that is essential for healing.

Motivates Meaningful Understanding

Recovery often involves complex emotions and challenges, and meaningful understanding is key to navigating these experiences. By fostering empathy, active listening, and genuine compassion, individuals can develop deeper connections with others and feel truly understood and supported on their journey.

Not Influence Change

In recovery, it's important to communicate authentically without trying to control or manipulate others. By respecting each individual's autonomy and journey, individuals can create a safe and supportive environment where everyone feels empowered to make their own choices and pursue their own path to recovery.

Trust Each Other

Trust is essential for building strong, healthy relationships, especially during the recovery process. By fostering trust through honesty, reliability, and mutual respect, individuals can create a supportive network of friends, family, and peers who are committed to each other's well-being and success.

No matter the challenges individuals face during recovery, whether it's overcoming addiction, coping with loss, or rebuilding after a setback, effective communication based on the principles of COMMUNICATE can foster connection, understanding, and trust, creating a solid foundation for healing and growth.

HEALTHY
COMMUNICATION
IS A
KEY TO
RECOVERY

Day 6

D.O.U.B.T

"NO MORE DOUBT"

Destroying Opportunities Utilizing Bad Thinking

While DOUBT may seem like a negative concept, acknowledging and addressing doubts can be valuable during the recovery journey:

Destroying Opportunities
Doubt has the potential to undermine progress and derail recovery efforts. By recognizing and confronting doubts head-on, individuals can prevent self-sabotage and avoid falling back into harmful patterns or behaviors that may hinder their recovery

Utilizing Bad Thinking
Negative thought patterns can be detrimental to recovery, leading to feelings of hopelessness and discouragement. By acknowledging and challenging these negative thoughts, individuals

can replace them with more positive and empowering beliefs, fostering resilience and optimism in the face of adversity.

In recovery, it's important to acknowledge the presence of doubt and negative thinking without allowing them to dictate one's actions or beliefs. By addressing doubts and negative thoughts in a constructive manner, individuals can cultivate inner strength, resilience, and confidence in their ability to overcome challenges and build a fulfilling life beyond addiction, loss, or hardship

Words have POWER be mindful of what you say to yourself, doubt and recovery DO NOT complement each other.

Day 7

F.E.A.R

"I have
Conquered
all of my
Fear"

Face Everything And Recover FEAR, when viewed as an acronym for "Face Everything And Recover," embodies a powerful message of courage and resilience during the recovery process

Face Everything
Recovery often requires confronting difficult emotions, memories, and challenges head-on. By facing everything with courage and honesty, individuals can gain a deeper understanding of themselves and their circumstances, paving the way for healing and growth.

And Recover
Recovery is not just about overcoming past traumas or setbacks; it's also about embracing the journey of healing and transformation. By committing to recovery and taking proactive

steps towards positive change, individuals can reclaim their lives and build a brighter future for themselves.

No matter the obstacles individuals face during recovery, whether it's addiction, loss, or other hardships, embracing the principles of FEAR can empower them to confront their fears, overcome challenges, and emerge stronger and more resilient than ever before. By facing everything with courage and determination, individuals can embark on a journey of recovery that leads to healing, growth, and ultimately, a life filled with hope and possibility.

Words of Encouragement

It's been 7 days, take a moment to reflect on the journey. It's been a very emotional week filled with times you felt like giving up, however you remained disciplined and consistent; at this point you're beginning to believe. Remember to celebrate your wins and constantly remind yourself, when needed, you can do this work without being hard on yourself. Smile ●

Week 2 will give you an opportunity to build on this momentum, studies shows it takes 21-30 days to formulate new habits and you're off to a great start. There is **NO REPLACEMENT** for doing the work; you can't buy **RECOVERY**.

CELEBRATE
YOUR
ACCOMPLISHMENTS

Day 8

G.R.A.T.I.T.U.D.E.

"I am grateful"

Give Respect As Though It's The Ultimate Displayed Expression

Give Respect
Gratitude encourages individuals to acknowledge and appreciate the support, guidance, and resources available to them during their recovery journey. By giving respect to themselves and others, individuals cultivate a sense of worthiness and connection that strengthens their resolve to overcome challenges.

As Though It's The Ultimate Displayed Expression
Gratitude is a powerful expression of appreciation for the blessings and opportunities in one's life, even amidst adversity. By embracing

gratitude as the ultimate expression of respect and appreciation, individuals can shift their focus from what they lack to what they have, fostering a sense of abundance and fulfillment.

During recovery, whether from addiction, loss, or other hardships, practicing gratitude can provide a source of strength and resilience. By acknowledging the support of others, recognizing the progress they've made, and finding gratitude in even the smallest blessings, individuals can cultivate a positive mindset that empowers them to navigate the challenges of recovery with grace and determination.

Learning how to be grateful for the little things helps on the recovery journey. It could always be worst, take a moment and write down 3 things that you are grateful for.

Day 9

H.O.P.E

> "Hope is belief that I am Able"

Having Only Positive Expectations

HOPE serves as a beacon of light and resilience during the recovery journey:

Having Only Positive Expectations
In the face of adversity, maintaining a positive outlook can be a powerful catalyst for change. By focusing on positive outcomes and possibilities, individuals in recovery can cultivate hope, resilience, and motivation to overcome challenges.

No matter the obstacles individuals face during recovery, whether it's addiction, loss, or other hardships, embracing the principle of HOPE can empower them to navigate the journey with optimism and determination. By believing in the possibility of a brighter future and holding onto positive expectations, individuals can tap into their inner strength and resilience, paving the way for healing, growth, and ultimately, a life filled with hope and possibility.

H ♡
P E

Day 10

S.H.I.F.T

"I am shifting into NEW habits"

Start Helping Individuals Follow Through

SHIFT embodies the essence of support and accountability, offering valuable guidance during the recovery process:

Start Helping
Recovery often requires a support system to provide encouragement, guidance, and assistance along the way. By starting the journey with help from friends, family, or professionals, individuals can access the resources and support they need to navigate the challenges of recovery successfully.

Individuals Follow Through
Recovery is a journey that requires commitment and perseverance. By providing support and encouragement, individuals can help those in recovery stay focused and motivated to follow

through with their goals and commitments, even when faced with obstacles or setbacks.

No matter the challenges individuals face during recovery, whether it's addiction, loss, or other hardships, embracing the principle of SHIFT can empower them to stay on track and achieve their goals. By starting the journey with support and assistance and helping individuals follow through with their commitments, we can create a community that fosters healing, growth, and resilience for all.

Day 11

D.E.N.I.A.L

"Living in my Truth"

Don't Even No I Am Lying

DENIAL, when understood as "Don't Even No I Am Lying," sheds light on the importance of recognizing and confronting denial during the recovery journey:

Don't Even No
Denial often involves avoiding or ignoring the reality of one's situation. By acknowledging the presence of denial, individuals can begin to break through the barriers that prevent them from seeing the truth about their behaviors, emotions, or circumstances.

I Am Lying
Denial is often rooted in self-deception and dishonesty. By acknowledging the lies they tell themselves and others, individuals can start to

unravel the layers of denial and begin to accept responsibility for their actions and choices.

During recovery, whether from addiction, loss, or other hardships, confronting denial is a crucial step towards healing and growth. By acknowledging the presence of denial, individuals can begin to dismantle the barriers that stand in the way of their recovery journey, paving the way for greater self-awareness, accountability, and ultimately, transformation.

Day 12

E.M.O.T.I.O.N

"Regulating my emotions brings freedom"

Relentless Energy Movement Obtained Through Intelligence Over Negativity

EMOTION represents a powerful force for transformation and healing during the recovery journey:

Relentless Energy
Emotions are a source of boundless energy that can drive individuals forward on their path to recovery. By harnessing this energy and channeling it into positive outlets such as self-care, creativity, or advocacy, individuals can fuel their journey with purpose and determination.

Movement Obtained Through Intelligence
Recovery requires a combination of self-awareness and informed decision-making. By using intelligence and critical thinking skills to

understand their emotions and triggers, individuals can make informed choices that support their recovery goals and promote long-term well-being.

Over Negativity

Embracing positive emotions and attitudes is essential for overcoming the challenges of recovery. By cultivating optimism, gratitude, and resilience, individuals can counteract negative thought patterns and emotions that may hinder their progress, leading to greater emotional balance and well-being.

During recovery, whether from addiction, loss, or other hardships, embracing the principles of EMOTION can empower individuals to navigate their emotions with resilience, intelligence, and positivity. By harnessing the energy of their emotions, making informed choices, and cultivating a positive mindset, individuals can tap into their inner strength and resilience, paving the way for healing, growth, and ultimately, a life filled with purpose and fulfillment.

Day 13

M.I.S.T.A.K.E.S

I am
overcoming
my mistakes

My Ignorance Suggests That Additional
Knowledge Employs Success

MISTAKES, when viewed through the lens of "My
Ignorance Suggests That Additional Knowledge
Employs Success," underscores the importance
of learning and growth during the recovery
journey:

My Ignorance
Mistakes often stem from a lack of awareness or
understanding. By acknowledging areas where
they may lack knowledge or insight, individuals
in recovery can begin to identify patterns of
behavior or thought that may be hindering their
progress.

Suggests That Additional Knowledge
Recovery is a journey of continuous learning and
growth. By embracing the opportunity to acquire

withstand challenges and setbacks with courage and resilience â€" individuals can navigate the ups and downs of recovery with determination and resilience..

Employs Success
Mistakes can serve as valuable learning opportunities that ultimately contribute to success. By reframing mistakes as steppingstones rather than setbacks, individuals can cultivate resilience, adaptability, and perseverance, qualities that are essential for long-term recovery and personal growth.

During recovery, whether from addiction, loss, or other hardships, embracing the principles of MISTAKES can empower individuals to approach challenges with curiosity, openness, and a willingness to learn. By recognizing the potential for growth inherent in every mistake, individuals can transform setbacks into opportunities for self-discovery, healing, and ultimately, success in their recovery journey.

Day 14

S.E.C.U.R.E

I am Secure

Stop Entertaining Childishness. Understand Real Endurance

SECURE serves as a reminder to cultivate maturity and resilience during the recovery journey:

Stop Entertaining Childishness
Recovery requires individuals to let go of behaviors or attitudes that no longer serve their well-being. By ceasing to entertain childish impulses or distractions, individuals can focus their energy on constructive activities and self-improvement, fostering personal growth and maturity.

Understand Real Endurance
Recovery is not a quick fix but a journey of endurance and perseverance. By understanding the true meaning of endurance - the ability to

withstand challenges and setbacks with courage and resilience - individuals can navigate the ups and downs of recovery with determination and resilience.

During recovery, whether from addiction, loss, or other hardships, embracing the principles of SECURE can empower individuals to cultivate maturity, resilience, and inner strength. By letting go of childish impulses and embracing the endurance required for long-term recovery, individuals can build a solid foundation for lasting healing and growth.

Words of Encouragement

It's been 14 days and it's starting to make sense. You're having more desire to work on the areas that have been identified as problematic. It's becoming easier to process information including how you feel, which I believe is crucial when it comes to RECOVERY.

There is NO turning back, we are committed to making change happen. This is becoming a new way of living and although it is difficult at times you're beginning to "trust the process".

Take a moment as you reflect to celebrate this milestone. It's all about YOU and YOUR Recovery journey.

EVERY
WIN
COUNTS

Day 15

L.O.V.E

"I am
loveable"

Living On Vibrational Energy

LOVE encapsulates the transformative power of positive energy during the recovery journey:

Living On Vibrational Energy
Recovery is not just about physical healing but also about nurturing one's emotional and spiritual well-being. By surrounding themselves with positive influences and experiences, individuals can raise their vibrational energy and create an environment that supports their healing and growth.

During recovery, whether from addiction, loss, or other hardships, embracing the principles of LOVE can empower individuals to cultivate a sense of inner peace, connection, and well-being. By living on vibrational energy and surrounding themselves with love and positivity, individuals can tap into their inner strength and resilience, paving the way for lasting healing and transformation.

What
Is
Love?

Day 16

I.N.C.R.E.A.S.E

"Increasing Knowledge creates an open mind"

Identifying Needed Change Requires Effectively Acknowledging Self-Error

INCREASE highlights the importance of self-awareness and accountability during the recovery journey:

Identifying Needed Change
Recovery begins with recognizing areas of one's life that require change or improvement. By identifying these areas, individuals can set meaningful goals and create a roadmap for their recovery journey.

Requires Effectively Acknowledging Self-Error
Recovery involves acknowledging past mistakes and taking responsibility for one's actions. By effectively acknowledging self-errors, individuals

can learn from their experiences, grow in self-awareness, and make positive changes to their behavior and mindset.

During recovery, whether from addiction, loss, or other hardships, embracing the principles of INCREASE can empower individuals to take ownership of their recovery journey. By identifying areas for change, acknowledging past mistakes, and committing to personal growth, individuals can increase their chances of success and create a life filled with purpose, fulfillment, and well-being.

Day 17

G.O.D

"I can accept what I can't change"

Gracefully Obeying Destiny

LAUGHTER serves as a powerful tool for healing and resilience during the recovery journey:

Live And Unapologetically
Recovery is about embracing life fully and authentically, without reservations or apologies. By living unapologetically, individuals can cultivate a sense of self-acceptance and authenticity, which are essential for building resilience and maintaining sobriety or coping with loss.

Grace Hearts That Embrace Reality
Recovery often requires individuals to confront difficult emotions and realities. By embracing these challenges with grace and compassion, individuals can cultivate a sense of acceptance

and resilience that enables them to navigate the ups and downs of recovery with greater ease.

During recovery, whether from addiction, loss, or other hardships, embracing the principles of LAUGHTER can empower individuals to find joy, connection, and meaning in their journey. By living unapologetically and embracing reality with grace and humor, individuals can cultivate resilience, build supportive relationships, and create a life filled with laughter, love, and fulfillment.

Day 18

L.A.U.G.H.T.E.R

"Laughter is therapeutic"

Live And Unapologetically Grace Hearts That Embrace Reality!

LAUGHTER serves as a powerful tool for healing and resilience during the recovery journey:

Live And Unapologetically
Recovery is about embracing life fully and authentically, without reservations or apologies. By living unapologetically, individuals can cultivate a sense of self-acceptance and authenticity, which are essential for building resilience and maintaining sobriety or coping with loss.

Grace Hearts That Embrace Reality
Recovery often requires individuals to confront difficult emotions and realities. By embracing these challenges with grace and compassion, individuals can cultivate a sense of acceptance

and resilience that enables them to navigate the ups and downs of recovery with greater ease.

During recovery, whether from addiction, loss, or other hardships, embracing the principles of LAUGHTER can empower individuals to find joy, connection, and meaning in their journey. By living unapologetically and embracing reality with grace and humor, individuals can cultivate resilience, build supportive relationships, and create a life filled with laughter, love, and fulfillment.

Day 19

H.U.M.B.L.E

"Humility leds to cleansing"

Healing Understanding Marveled By Love Eternally

HUMBLE embodies the essence of humility and love, offering profound support during the recovery journey:

Healing
Recovery is a journey of healing, both physically and emotionally. By embracing humility, individuals can open themselves up to the healing process, allowing themselves to be vulnerable and receptive to support and guidance from others.

Understanding
Recovery requires individuals to gain insight into their thoughts, emotions, and behaviors. By approaching their journey with humility and an open mind, individuals can cultivate a deeper

understanding of themselves and their circumstances, empowering them to make positive changes and overcome challenges.

Marveled By Love Eternally

Love is a powerful force that sustains us through our darkest moments and fuels our journey towards recovery. By humbly accepting the love and support of others, individuals can find strength, hope, and resilience to navigate the ups and downs of recovery with grace and courage.

During recovery, whether from addiction, loss, or other hardships, embracing the principles of HUMBLE can empower individuals to cultivate a deeper sense of self-awareness, resilience, and connection to others. By approaching their journey with humility and love, individuals can create a supportive environment that fosters healing, growth, and ultimately, a life filled with joy, purpose, and fulfillment.

Day 20

I.N.S.P.I.R.A.T.I.O.N

"I am inspired to change my life"

I'll Never Stop Progressing, Instead Rise Above the Idea of Negativity

INSPIRATION serves as a guiding light during the recovery journey, encouraging individuals to embrace progress and positivity:

I'll Never Stop Progressing
Recovery is an ongoing journey of growth and self-improvement. By adopting a mindset of continuous progress, individuals can remain committed to their recovery goals and continually strive to become the best version of themselves.

Instead Rise Above the Idea of Negativity
Recovery often involves overcoming negative thought patterns and self-limiting beliefs. By choosing to rise above negativity and focus on positive possibilities, individuals can cultivate

resilience and optimism, empowering them to overcome challenges and setbacks on their journey to recovery.

During recovery, whether from addiction, loss, or other hardships, embracing the principles of INSPIRATION can empower individuals to stay motivated, focused, and resilient. By embracing progress and positivity, individuals can tap into their inner strength and determination, paving the way for lasting healing, growth, and fulfillment.

Day 21

F.R.I.E.N.D

"How
many of
us have
them?"

Fabulous Refreshing Intentional Enduring Nurturing Defender

FRIEND embodies the essence of supportive relationships during the recovery journey:

Fabulous
Friends bring joy, laughter, and positivity into our lives. During recovery, having fabulous friends who uplift and encourage us can provide invaluable support and motivation to stay on track and overcome challenges.

Refreshing
True friends offer a refreshing perspective and help us see things in a new light. Their support and guidance can provide clarity and inspiration, helping us navigate the complexities of recovery with renewed energy and enthusiasm.

Intentional

Friends who are intentional in their support are invaluable during recovery. They listen without judgment, offer practical help and encouragement, and hold us accountable to our goals, helping us stay focused and motivated on our journey to healing.

Enduring

True friendship withstands the test of time and adversity. During recovery, having enduring friends who stand by us through thick and thin can provide a sense of stability, security, and belonging, helping us weather the ups and downs of the recovery journey with grace and resilience.

Nurturing

Friends who nurture our well-being and growth are essential during recovery. They offer empathy, compassion, and understanding, creating a safe and supportive environment where we can heal, grow, and thrive.

Defender

Friends who defend and protect our well-being are like guardians during recovery. They stand up for us, advocate on our behalf, and provide a sense of safety and security, helping us feel valued, respected, and supported as we navigate the challenges of recovery.

Words of Encouragement

After 21 days of being consistent and disciplined, you have begun to formulate a new habit. Journaling allows us to process feelings and emotions through visualization of writing it down. Your at the stage where using journaling as a tool helps you identify problems and solutions faster. The first step in change is identifying the issue, journaling allows you to map out the endless possibilities.

This is a HUGE accomplishment and I want you to take a moment to congratulate yourself, This victory reinforces that when you put in the work that changes are possible.

RECOVERY
REQUIRES
DOING THE
WORK

Day 22

G.R.A.T.I.T.U.D.E

"Gratefulness is next to Godliness"

Give Respect As Though It's The Ultimate Displayed Expression

Give Respect
Gratitude encourages individuals to acknowledge and appreciate the support, guidance, and resources available to them during their recovery journey. By giving respect to themselves and others, individuals cultivate a sense of worthiness and connection that strengthens their resolve to overcome challenges.

As Though It's The Ultimate Displayed Expression
Gratitude is a powerful expression of appreciation for the blessings and opportunities in one's life, even amidst adversity. By embracing

gratitude as the ultimate expression of respect and appreciation, individuals can shift their focus from what they lack to what they have, fostering a sense of abundance and fulfillment.

During recovery, whether from addiction, loss, or other hardships, practicing gratitude can provide a source of strength and resilience. By acknowledging the support of others, recognizing the progress they've made, and finding gratitude in even the smallest blessings, individuals can cultivate a positive mindset that empowers them to navigate the challenges of recovery with grace and determination.

Learning how to be grateful for the little things helps on the recovery journey. It could always be worst, take a moment and write down 3 things that you are grateful for.

Day 23

E.G.O

"My ego
has
landed"

Edging God Out

Understanding the concept of EGO, or "Edging God Out," can be valuable during the recovery journey:

Edging God Out
The ego often leads individuals to prioritize their own desires, fears, and insecurities over their connection to something greater than themselves, whether it's a higher power, spirituality, or the support of a community. By recognizing when the ego is in control, individuals can begin to release its grip and open themselves up to the guidance, strength, and support that comes from surrendering to a higher power or seeking support from others.

During recovery, whether from addiction, loss, or other hardships, acknowledging and addressing

During recovery, whether from addiction, loss, or other hardships, having FRIENDs who embody these qualities can make all the difference in our journey to healing and transformation. They offer not only companionship and support but also inspiration, encouragement, and hope for a brighter future ahead.

Day 24

H.E.L.P

"I am able to ask for help"

Honorable Encouragement Linking Purpose

HELP embodies the essence of support and guidance during the recovery journey:

Honorable
Offering help with honor means providing support with integrity, respect, and empathy. Honorable assistance acknowledges the dignity and worth of individuals in recovery, empowering them to navigate their journey with strength and dignity.

Encouragement
Recovery often requires individuals to overcome obstacles and setbacks. Encouragement provides individuals with motivation, inspiration, and belief in their ability to overcome challenges and achieve their goals, fostering resilience and determination.

Linking Purpose

Help that links individuals to their purpose can be invaluable during recovery. By connecting individuals to their values, passions, and aspirations, meaningful assistance provides a sense of direction, meaning, and fulfillment, empowering individuals to stay focused on their recovery journey.

During recovery, whether from addiction, loss, or other hardships, offering HELP that is honorable, encouraging, and linked to purpose can make a profound difference in an individual's journey to healing and transformation. It provides the support, guidance, and motivation individuals need to overcome challenges, build resilience, and reclaim their lives with purpose and meaning.

Day 25

P.E.A.C.E

"I have peace within me"

Positive Energy Always Corrects Errors

PEACE embodies the transformative power of positivity and self-correction during the recovery journey:

Positive Energy
Positivity is one of the catalysts for change and growth during recovery. By cultivating positive energy, individuals can shift their mindset from one of defeat to one of hope and resilience, enabling them to overcome challenges and setbacks with grace and determination.

Always Corrects Errors
Recovery often involves confronting past mistakes and learning from them. By embracing a mindset of self-correction, individuals can acknowledge their errors, take responsibility for their actions, and make positive changes that

support their journey to healing and recovery.

During recovery, whether from addiction, loss, or other hardships, embodying the principles of PEACE can empower individuals to find inner tranquility, strength, and resilience. By embracing positivity and self-correction, individuals can navigate the challenges of recovery with grace and determination, ultimately finding peace within themselves and their journey towards healing and wholeness.

Day 26

L.I.G.H.T

"I am light
and have
no fear"

Lift Ignite Gifting Healing Tranquility

LIGHT represents the transformative power of positivity and healing during the recovery journey:

Lift
Recovery often begins with a lifting of burdens, whether, emotional, or spiritual. By lifting the weight of past traumas, regrets, and fears, individuals can free themselves to embark on a journey of healing, growth, and self-discovery.

Ignite
Recovery ignites a spark of hope and possibility within individuals. By igniting this flame of resilience and determination, individuals can overcome challenges and setbacks with courage and perseverance, fueling their journey towards healing and transformation.

Gifting

Recovery is a gift, offering individuals the opportunity to reclaim their lives and pursue their dreams. By embracing this gift with gratitude and humility, individuals can cultivate a sense of appreciation for the blessings and opportunities that come with recovery, empowering them to make the most of each day.

Healing

Recovery is a journey of healing, both physically and emotionally. By embracing the process of healing with patience, compassion, and self-care, individuals can nurture their well-being and cultivate inner peace, resilience, and wholeness.

Tranquility

Recovery ultimately leads to a sense of inner tranquility and peace. By embracing the principles of recovery, individuals can find solace and serenity amidst life's challenges, knowing that they have the strength, resilience, and support to overcome whatever obstacles come their way.

During recovery, whether from addiction, loss, or other hardships, embodying the principles of LIGHT can empower individuals to find hope, healing, and tranquility in their journey towards recovery. By lifting burdens, igniting hope, embracing gratitude, nurturing healing, and finding inner peace, individuals can illuminate their path towards a brighter, more fulfilling future.

THERE IS
LIGHT
IN THE
DARKNESS

Day 27

P.E.R.S.E.V.E.R.E

"I am sticking to it"

Persistence Evolution Relaxation Stability Energetic Vibrant Elimination Rough Edges

PERSEVERE embodies the qualities essential for navigating the challenges of recovery:

Persistence
Recovery requires unwavering persistence and determination. By persisting through difficult moments and setbacks, individuals can stay focused on their goals and continue making progress towards healing and growth.

Evolution
Recovery is a journey of personal evolution and transformation. By embracing change and growth, individuals can evolve into their best selves, learning from their experiences and becoming stronger, wiser, and more resilient along the way.

Relaxation
Recovery involves finding moments of rest and relaxation amidst the journey. By prioritizing self-care and relaxation techniques such as mindfulness, meditation, or hobbies, individuals can recharge their energy and reduce stress, enhancing their overall well-being and resilience.

Stability
Recovery often involves establishing stability in various areas of life, such as relationships, finances, and daily routines. By cultivating stability, individuals can create a solid foundation for their recovery journey, reducing uncertainty and fostering a sense of security and confidence.

Energetic
Recovery requires a vibrant energy and zest for life. By embracing activities and practices that energize and uplift them, individuals can maintain a positive mindset and attitude, fueling their journey towards healing and transformation.

Vibrant
Recovery is about embracing life fully and vibrantly. By cultivating joy, passion, and enthusiasm for life, individuals can infuse their recovery journey with vitality and purpose, inspiring themselves and others along the way.

Elimination of Rough Edges

Recovery involves confronting and addressing the rough edges of one's past and present. By acknowledging and working through challenges and unresolved issues, individuals can smooth out these rough edges, fostering greater emotional and psychological well-being.

During recovery, whether from addiction, loss, or other hardships, embodying the principles of PERSEVERE can empower individuals to stay resilient, focused, and optimistic on their journey towards healing and wholeness. By persisting through challenges, evolving into their best selves, prioritizing self-care and stability, maintaining vibrant energy and enthusiasm, and addressing rough edges, individuals can navigate the complexities of recovery with grace, courage, and strength.

Day 28

D.E.D.I.C.A.T.E

"I am dedicated to my recovery"

Determine Excited Delighted Ignited Confident Alive Thrilled Electrifying

DEDICATE embodies the spirit of commitment and enthusiasm crucial for success in the recovery journey:

Determine
Recovery requires a strong determination to overcome obstacles and achieve goals. By setting intentions and staying focused on their recovery journey, individuals can navigate challenges with resilience and perseverance.

Excited
Embracing excitement for the possibilities of recovery can fuel motivation and optimism. By cultivating a sense of excitement for the positive changes ahead, individuals can approach their recovery journey with enthusiasm and hope.

Delighted

Finding joy and delight in the process of recovery can enhance well-being and resilience. By celebrating small victories and milestones along the way, individuals can reinforce their commitment to recovery and stay motivated during difficult times.

Ignited

Recovery ignites a spark of transformation and growth within individuals. By embracing this sense of inner fire and passion, individuals can tap into their innate potential and harness their energy towards positive change and healing.

Confident

Confidence is essential for navigating the challenges of recovery. By cultivating self-belief and trusting in their abilities, individuals can face setbacks with resilience and approach their recovery journey with courage and determination.

Alive

Recovery is about rediscovering a sense of vitality and purpose in life. By embracing the present moment and connecting it with the joys of being alive, individuals can cultivate a deeper appreciation for life and find motivation to pursue their recovery goals.

Thrilled

Embracing a sense of thrill and adventure in the recovery journey can make the process more engaging and rewarding. By approaching challenges with curiosity and openness, individuals can discover new opportunities for growth and transformation.

Electrifying

Recovery has the potential to electrify individuals with newfound energy and enthusiasm for life. By embracing the electrifying energy of positive change, individuals can channel their excitement into their recovery journey, fueling their progress towards a brighter future.

During recovery, whether from addiction, loss, or other hardships, embodying the principles of DEDICATE can empower individuals to stay committed, enthusiastic, and resilient on their journey towards healing and transformation. By determining their goals, embracing excitement and delight, igniting their passion, fostering confidence and aliveness, and thrilling in the electrifying energy of positive change, individuals can navigate the recovery process with purpose, joy, and vitality.

.

Words of Encouragement

After completing 30 days we now have a new habit we can add to our recovery tool box. Recovery is a journey NOT a destination and requires discipline, commitment, consistency and most important TIME.

I am proud of you, more importantly be proud of yourself, Recovery for everyone is different and when you find something that works, work it.

Welcome to your new life filled with the ability to reflect and adjust. Emotions make you cry sometimes and that's ok. Now the real work begins on maintaining what you built.

Cheers to a new day, A new attitude, A new YOU!! Let's do it Again and Again this time bring a friend ●.

FLIGHT ATTENDANTS PREPARE THE CABIN FOR ARRIVAL

Day 29

H.A.B.I.T

> "I am creating good habits"

Healthy Attributes Becoming Intentionally True

HABIT embodies the transformational power of cultivating healthy habits during the recovery journey:

Healthy Attributes
Recovery involves adopting and nurturing positive attributes that contribute to overall well-being. By focusing on developing healthy habits such as regular exercise, nutritious eating, adequate sleep, and mindfulness practices, individuals can support their physical, emotional, and mental health, laying the foundation for a sustainable recovery.

Becoming Intentionally True
Recovery is about aligning one's actions and behaviors with their true values and aspirations. By becoming intentionally true to themselves,

individuals can cultivate authenticity, self-awareness, and self-acceptance, empowering them to make choices that honor their recovery journey and lead to personal growth and fulfillment.

During recovery, whether from addiction, loss, or other hardships, embracing the principles of HABIT can empower individuals to build a strong foundation for lasting change and well-being. By cultivating healthy habits and aligning their actions with their true selves, individuals can enhance their resilience, self-esteem, and sense of purpose, leading to a more fulfilling and meaningful life in recovery.

Day 30

P.A.T.H

"I am on
the path of
new life"

Purposefully Attuned to Hope

PATH represents the journey of recovery as a purposeful alignment with hope:

Purposefully
Recovery requires individuals to approach their journey with intention and purpose. By setting clear goals, making conscious choices, and taking deliberate actions, individuals can navigate their path towards healing and transformation with clarity and determination.

Attuned to Hope
Hope is a guiding light that illuminates the darkest moments of recovery. By remaining attuned to hope, individuals can cultivate resilience, optimism, and belief in the possibility of a brighter future, even in the face of adversity.

individuals can cultivate authenticity, self-awareness, and self-acceptance, empowering them to make choices that honor their recovery journey and lead to personal growth and fulfillment.

During recovery, whether from addiction, loss, or other hardships, embracing the principles of PATH can empower individuals to stay focused, resilient, and optimistic on their journey towards healing and wholeness. By purposefully aligning with hope and remaining attuned to its guiding presence, individuals can navigate the challenges of recovery with grace, courage, and strength, knowing that they are moving towards a brighter tomorrow.

Final Words of Encouragement

After completing 30 days we now have a new habit we can add to our recovery tool box. Recovery is a journey NOT a destination and requires discipline, commitment, consistency and most important TIME.

I am proud of you, more importantly be proud of yourself, Recovery for everyone is different and when you find something that works, work it.

Welcome to your new life filled with the ability to reflect and adjust. Emotions make you cry sometimes and that's ok. Now the real work begins on maintaining what you built.

Cheers to a new day, A new attitude, A new YOU!! Let's do it Again and Again this time bring a friend ●.

About The Author

Erick D. Allen Sr. was born in Portland, Oregon in a historically marginalized community. He takes pride in filling the void in the market place. His goal is to change the narrative on how counseling and therapy is presented and recieved, especially with people of color.

As a Certified Substance Abuse and Mental Health Counselor, Mr. Allen's is to uplift others through the diagnosis and treatment of addiction as a mental illness.

Throught journaling he was able to learn the art of unpacking trauma and how to use life experiences as a testimony of perseverance.

His motto is "Resiliency & Recovery- one individual, One family, and One Community at a time."

www.ingramcontent.com/pod-product-compliance
Lightning Source LLC
Chambersburg PA
CBHW070813280326
41934CB00012B/3177